Kingdom Finances

Kingdom Finances

40 Financial Principles That Empower You
to Properly Manage Money

Krystle Bell Saulsberry

Dedication

This book is dedicated to anyone who wants to shift their thinking and learn how to properly manage money in a manner that is pleasing to God.

Foreword

"Beloved, I wish above all things that thou mayest prosper and be in health even as your soul prospereth." (III John 1:2)

When I think of this scripture, my heart goes immediately to my goddaughter, Krystle Bell Saulsberry. In the many years that I have known her, I have seen an exact correlation of when her soul is at peace about particular matters, she financially prospers. Her response, as we see in III John, is truly biblical. I have come to find that prosperity is not simply financial prosperity. This outward manifestation if accompanied with good health, happiness, love and so on is the true embodiment of prosperity. This total prosperity is in my belief, is what we call, "peace". Some define it as, "Nothing missing and nothing broken." Each time Krystle does the "inner work" to attain peace, her life blossoms.

In her latest book, *Kingdom Finances: 40 Financial Principles That Empower You to Properly Manage Money*, we see God's handiwork of peace. Here, forty epiphanies from God directly to her spirit have come to bless the body of Christ and the common man. They were not simply epiphanies that required no work. One principle she shares sticks out like a sore thumb:

- You cannot wander out of debt.

Here Krystle is speaking the utter truth with the due diligence to have lived it. At 31 years old, she creatively worked her way completely out of debt. She turned off the cable television, brought lunch to work, and the list goes on. You truly cannot "wander out of debt". It takes a clear and concise plan along with a decision and action.

- Never rely on just one source of income.

Having worked with her for nine years, we often shared that the paycheck was simply seed but the "rivers" and "streams" of income were signs of financial prosperity.

This book is not lengthy but rather precious and golden nuggets that can be meditated on each day of the month. She blesses the young person looking for an example and the older generation like myself as well. I present to you: *Kingdom Finances: 40 Financial Principles That Empower You to Properly Manage Money.*

Twanna Walton
Krystle's Godmom

Preface

A few years ago, I started a segment on my personal Facebook page entitled "Financial Friday." During "Financial Friday", I would post quotes, sayings, and affirmations that catered to the topic of personal finance. These posts were designed to share my personal thoughts on the topic as well as empower others to shift their thinking about money.

I actually became interested in personal finance in March 2012 when I took Dave's Ramsey Financial Peace University class at Faith Church in Montgomery, Alabama. The class left a major impact upon me, and I made a decision then to change my life so that I could prosper in the area of finances. Those teachings helped me to change my thoughts and habits towards money, and I was able to become debt free in May 2016 at the age of 31. Since then, I have had the opportunity to teach personal finance classes to teens and adults, and I have helped them to understand the importance of saving, debt elimination, and giving to others.

Kingdom Finances: 40 Financial Principles That Empower You to Properly Manage Money was birthed from my "Financial Friday" posts. This short book of principles will help you shift your thinking so you can begin to live a life of financial abundance. A mental shift must first take place before real change can occur. Enjoy the journey.

Krystle Bell Saulsberry
November 2017
Oxford, Alabama

Table of Contents

Introduction

Are you tired of living paycheck to paycheck? Do you want to be your own boss? Do you want to become empowered to succeed financially? You can begin living the life you have always wanted if you are intentional and have the right mindset. I believe the reason why so many people struggle with money is because they have trained their brains to think negatively about it. Money, in itself, is not evil, but a tool designed to effect change in society. Money flows to those who understand it and to those who know how to handle it.

It is time to shift your thinking and modify your behavior so you can become financially prosperous. Kingdom Finances teaches key financial principles so you can begin to learn how to handle money in a way that is pleasing to God. These financial principles cover areas such as income, debt, savings, and giving. Meditate on these financial principles daily and watch how your mindset shifts. This mental shift will allow behavior modification to take place, and the door of prosperity will begin to open.

Kingdom Finances

Pay for things with cash or leave them at the store.

It is time out for relying on other people for your own success.

Do not rely on a job to take care of you.

Take control of your financial destiny, and start your own business. Do not make anyone else rich; make yourself rich.

The federal government cannot save you from your financial problems. Change your behavior, and you will see results.

You cannot wander out of debt.

Are you a giver? If not, you are not serious about being wealthy.

If you always buy things that go down in value, you will never be wealthy.

Your giving opens the door to prosperity.

People who are serious about their finances do not spend every dollar they make. Have some financial discipline for goodness sake.

Stay true to your financial principles regardless of other people's opinions.

Broke people make excuses and procrastinate. Wealthy people make a plan and execute.

Hoping for money is not going to make money appear. You have to do something about it. Get to work and stop waiting for a handout.

Living paycheck to paycheck is not God's best for your life. If you don't believe me, read John 10:10.

A large tax refund is not a surplus of money you receive during tax season. It is an interest free loan to the federal government. Check your withholdings, and stop letting the federal government hold your money interest free for a year.

If you have a lack of mindset, you will always have a lack of money. Poverty mindsets will get you nowhere.

A job is not your source;
God is your source.

Never rely on just one source of
income.

Debt plus a lack of discipline equals bondage.

The money will come when you are disciplined.

Do not rely on man to give you financial freedom.

God gives YOU the ability to make your own way prosperous.

If you have a need, get to work. Stop being lazy and start hustling.

Sometimes you have to JUMP in order to live out your true purpose in life. It will not be easy, and you will go through uncomfortable seasons. However, millionaires do not become millionaires by being comfortable and working for someone else. They have to take risks.

Mindlessly spending money is hazardous to your financial health.

When you have financial peace, you can do anything.

How you spend your money is a reflection of how you live your life.

Your faith has to be bigger than your bank account.

*A lack of money comes from
a lack of faith.*

*A budget is not designed to keep you
in bondage; it is designed to
keep you disciplined.*

An impoverished mind will never be able to attract wealth into your life.

A healthy mind is a wealthy mind.

Savings serves as an umbrella for the rainy days.

Credit cards provide a short-term solution for a long-term problem.

Tithing is God honoring.

You are the manager of God's money. Don't get fired from the job because of negligence and a lack of discipline.

Make God proud, and properly manage the things He has given you.

Attention to detail is crucial in succeeding financially.

Do not allow broke people to influence your financial decisions.

Examine yourself and make sure you are attracting the right people into your financial circle.

About the Author

Born and raised in Roanoke, Alabama, Krystle Bell Saulsberry is a 2007 magna cum laude graduate of Jacksonville State University with a Bachelor of Arts in Political Science and a double minor in Spanish/Business and Technical Writing. She is a 2011 graduate of Auburn University Montgomery with a Master of Public Administration with a concentration in Nonprofit Management and Leadership.

Krystle's journey in personal finance education began in March 2012 when she became a student of Dave Ramsey's Financial Peace University. Her drive, consistency, and discipline led her to becoming debt free at the age of 31 and becoming a full-time entrepreneur at the age of 32. She spends her time educating others on how to succeed in the area of personal finance. Affectionately known as "The Financial Queen," Krystle is also a certified life coach, professional pageant coach, and blogger. She is also the author of #1 Amazon.com bestselling book *Manifest the Crown: A Krystle Clear Guide to Pageantry Success.*